. . . I never saw another butterfly . . .

Children's Drawings and Poems
from Terezin Concentration Camp
1942–1944

Edited by Hana Volavková
Expanded Second Edition by the
United States Holocaust Memorial Museum

Foreword by Chaim Potok
Afterword by Vaclav Havel

SCHOCKEN BOOKS · NEW YORK

All rights reserved under International and Pan-American
Copyright Conventions. Published in the United States by
Schocken Books Inc., New York, and simultaneously in Canada
by Random House of Canada Limited, Toronto. Distributed by
Pantheon Books, a division of Random House, Inc., New York.

Originally published in a different form in a special edition for the State Jewish Museum
in Prague in 1959. A revised edition was published by Artia for Schocken Books in 1978.
Copyright © 1978 by Artia, Prague.
This new edition originally published by Schocken Books in hardcover in 1993.

Excerpts from the diary of Helga Weissová on pp. 22 and 24 and the drawing on p. 23
reprinted by permission of Helga Weissová-Hošková.

Library of Congress Cataloging-in-Publication Data

Dětské kresby na zastávce k smrti, Terezin, 1942–1944. English.
    I never saw another butterfly : children's drawings and poems from
  Terezin concentration camp, 1942–1944 / edited by Hana Volavková ;
  revised and expanded by the U.S. Holocaust Memorial Museum ; with a
  new foreword by Chaim Potok.
        p.   cm.
    Summary: A selection of children's poems and drawings reflecting
  their surroundings in Terezin Concentration Camp in Czechoslovakia
  from 1942 to 1944.
    ISBN 0-8052-1015-6
    1. Children's art.   2. Children's writings.   3. Terezin
  (Czechoslovakia : Concentration camp)   4. Concentration camps—
  Czechoslovakia.   [1. Children's art.   2. Children's writings.
  3. Terezin (Czechoslovakia : Concentration camp)   4. Concentration
  camps—Czechoslovakia.]   I. Volavková, Hana.   II. United States
  Holocaust Memorial Museum.   III. Title.
  N352.P713   1993
  741.9437′1—dc20   92-50477

Book design by Jo Anne Metsch
Manufactured in Japan
Revised Schocken Paperback Edition 1994
9 8 7 6 5 4 3 2 1

CONTENTS

A NOTE FROM THE UNITED STATES
HOLOCAUST MEMORIAL MUSEUM

In 1989, the State Jewish Museum in Prague entered into a cooperative agreement to loan the United States Holocaust Memorial Museum twenty-four original drawings and to permit the museum to make fifty facsimiles of original works by the children of Terezin for display in an exhibit on children in the Holocaust. The children's exhibit, which includes artifacts from the concentration camp/ghetto at Terezin, is part of a permanent exhibition on display at the museum in Washington, D.C.

The United States Holocaust Memorial Museum is the national memorial to the victims of the Holocaust. Chartered by a unanimous act of Congress and built on federal land with private funds donated by the American people, the museum has three components: a museum to tell the story of the Holocaust, a memorial to its victims, and educational programs with a moral mission.

This unique institution is an educational and historical museum. The artifacts, films, photographs, and documents presented in the museum's permanent exhibition tell the story of the Holocaust, beginning with the Nazi assumption of power in 1933 and concluding with the resettlement of survivors in the United States and Israel. Among the museum's important artifacts are a rail car of the type used to transport Jews from Warsaw to Treblinka, a barracks from Birkenau, and a Danish fishing boat that was used to ferry Jews to safety in Sweden. Some of the most cherished artifacts to be found in the museum are twenty-four original artworks from Theresienstadt along with fifty handmade facsimiles of the originals. These works of art—remnants of the lives of the children who drew them—will form the core of a major exhibit on the fate of the over one million Jewish children murdered by the Nazis.

The museum is also an educational institution to be visited by schoolchildren traveling with their teachers and by children accompanied by their parents. In addition to its permanent exhibition, the museum presents an exhibition especially designed for elementary-school stu-

dents entitled "Remember the Children," which portrays the experience of children during the Holocaust.

The opening of the museum in April 1993 and these exhibits have provided the opportunity to present an expanded edition of *I Never Saw Another Butterfly*, the well-known collection of poems and drawings by the children in Terezin.

The original edition of *Butterfly*, edited by Hana Volavková and translated by Jeanne Nemcová, was published in the United States in 1964 and reprinted by Schocken Books in 1978. This new, expanded edition includes all the material selected by Mrs. Volavková, with additional illustrations and additional poems translated by Arnost Lustig, Vera Weislitz Lustig, and Elizabeth Rees. Excerpts from the diary of Helga Weissová, included by permission of Helga Weissová-Hosková, record specific events at Terezin remembered by all its surviving inmates. The Afterword written for this edition by Vaclav Havel, the former President of Czechoslovakia, was translated by Rita Klimová, the Czechoslovakian Ambassador to the United States.

The children of Terezin left a remarkable legacy in their poetry and art. No less remarkable were the teachers who defied camp rules to offer the children art therapy in the guise of art lessons, to teach literature, and to organize poetry contests, recitations, and cultural programs in the girls' and boys' dormitories. One such teacher was Friedl Dicker-Brandeis. A former student of the Bauhaus in Weimar, Germany, she was an accomplished artist, designer, and teacher. When she was ordered to Terezin in December 1942, she conceived a mission for herself and brought what art materials she could to the camp.

Mrs. Dicker-Brandeis saw that the children of Terezin needed a form of artistic expression as a way to moderate the chaos of their lives. Drawing on her Bauhaus experience and available supplies—her hoarded materials, office forms, scrap paper, cardboard, wrapping paper—she provided excellent training in art fundamentals, studies of everyday objects, imaginative drawing, and complex still lifes, all the while freeing her students to reveal their feelings through their art.

One of her students, Raja Engländerová, recalled in her memoirs: "I remember Mrs. Brandeis as a tender, highly intelligent woman, who managed—for some hours every week—to create a fairy world for us

in Terezin . . . a world that made us forget all the surrounding hardships that we were not spared despite our young ages."

In most cases, little is known about the children of Terezin. Camp records generally provided only dates of birth; arrival at Terezin; and departure, destination, and fate. The Catalog of Drawings and the Catalog of Poems in this book provide what information is available. Many of the works were unsigned and thus the names of their young creators are unknown.

"Art constantly challenges the process by which the individual person is reduced to anonymity," writes the Israeli novelist Aharon Appelfeld, himself a child survivor of the Holocaust. Through their artistic expressions, the voices of these children, each one unique and individual, reach us across the abyss of the greatest crime in human history, allow us to touch them, and restore our own humanity in doing so.

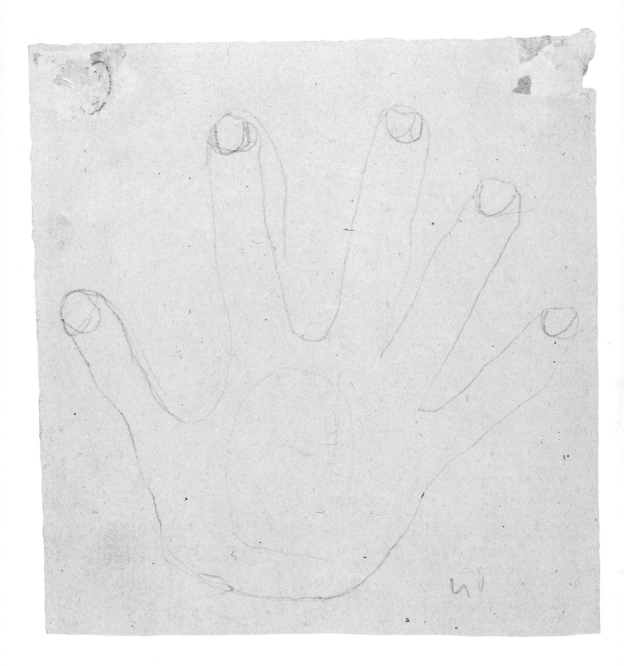

FOREWORD
by Chaim Potok

In the year 1780, near the site in the central mountains of Bohemia where the Elbe flows into the Ohre, the Hapsburg emperor Joseph II built a fortress—a walled garrison town—that he named for his mother, Maria Theresa. It lay nestled at the confluence of the two rivers: thick octagon-shaped walls, high escarpments, deep moats; narrow streets joined at right angles, homes dark and bleak, huge gray barracks. A fortress town set in a serene world of meadows and low rolling hills and summer butterflies against a distant background of bluish Bohemian mountains.

The Czechs called the town Terezin.

Eventually it became a civilian town, never housing more than 8,000 people. About 50 percent of its population consisted of soldiers. Even the 98 Czech Jews who lived there in 1930 were mostly soldiers.

The town was spared direct attack; enemies simply went around it. In early 1941, its inhabitants, including 10 Jewish families, numbered 3,700 individuals.

Nearby stood another, smaller fortress: a prison, with isolation cells, a yard for a firing squad, and a gallows.

Early in 1939, German troops crossed the Czech frontier and marched into Prague. Bohemia and Moravia were made German protectorates. Czechoslovakia was dismembered and absorbed into the Greater Reich.

In October 1941, Terezin became Theresienstadt, a ghetto, to be administered by the SS, guarded by Czech gendarmes, and run internally by a Jewish Council of Elders.

The Theresienstadt ghetto was created by the Germans to solve an awkward problem they had unexpectedly come upon in their war against the Jews: what to do with certain special categories of Jews.

It is fairly common knowledge by now that Nazi Germany saw itself engaged in two major wars simultaneously: one, profane; the other, from the German point of view, holy.

The first was the war against the liberal democracies and communism;

the second—in many ways fought more tenaciously and with far more ruthlessness than the first—was the war against European Jewry. That second war was not a peripheral struggle undertaken by Nazi thugs, nor was it decided upon after the Nazis rose to power. It was core Nazi ideology, a mission Nazism took upon itself as a sacred duty from its very beginnings.

Antisemitism—hatred of the Jews—is blatantly present in the earliest writings of Hitler, who made his intent clear in *Mein Kampf:* "I believe that I am acting in the spirit of Almighty God; in defending myself from the Jews, I am doing God's work." It is present as well in his speeches during the 1930s, and in his last testament. The order to "continue the fight against the pest"—that is, Jewry—was given as part of his final legacy before he committed suicide in April 1945.

Nazism entered the world with a clear and unambiguous hatred of the Jews. But the response to the problem of what to do with the Jews underwent a gradual process of evolution.

The early Nazi policies regarding German Jews—isolation, expulsion, emigration—proved a clear success. Of the 500,000 Jews in Germany when Hitler took power in 1933, about 320,000 had emigrated by 1939. By the start of the Second World War, the remaining Jews of Germany, as well as those in the Greater Reich, had been effectively ostracized from the new society created by the National Socialist system.

When the war began, the Nazis had no clearly formulated plans for the Jews of Europe. A number of conquered local governments—Vichy France, as an example—segregated their Jewish populations even before the Germans ordered it. All through Eastern Europe, local police and German troops herded Jews into areas newly designated as ghettos (there had been no ghettos in Eastern Europe until then). The Jews were being made ready for some further step in a developing design the outlines of which were not yet clear.

Then, in June 1941, Germany invaded the Soviet Union, and at about that time Hitler's policy toward the Jews seemed to take on a sudden, sharp focus. The precise sequence of events leading to his final decision is still unclear. Was the plan Hitler's alone? Did he arrive at it together with others? Documentation is fuzzy; historians are uncertain.

This much is clear: In the late summer or early fall of 1941, the Nazis determined to kill every living Jew they could lay their hands on. On

October 28, 1941, the Gestapo issued a decree: Jews were henceforth prohibited from leaving Europe. The Final Solution—the Nazi term for the extermination of the Jews—had begun.

The first mass killing grounds were in the Soviet Union. Special units accompanied the German Army; their specific mission: Liquidate Jews. Between 800,000 and one million Jews died at their hands.

One can trace with ease the steps taken by the Nazi implementers of the Final Solution as they proceeded from the use of special units in the Soviet Union, which proved too cumbersome and public a process, to the construction of special sites: camps for technological mass annihilation.

Addressing his lieutenant generals at a meeting in Poznan on October 4, 1943, Heinrich Himmler, head of the Nazi SS, said, "It has been an appalling task for us to kill the Jewish people." Only the SS, he went on, understood what it meant "to see a hundred corpses, or five hundred, or a thousand, lying side by side." They could never speak of it publicly. "This is a page of glory in our history that is never to be written. . . . We had the moral right, we had the duty to destroy this people, who wanted to destroy us. . . . We have exterminated a germ. . . ."

Two mysteries lie at the heart of the Nazi war against the Jews.

First, what was it about the Germans that so set them against the Jews? More specifically, how did it happen that in the mind and heart of one man, Adolf Hitler, there could rise so incendiary a hatred toward a people other than his own that it could be assuaged only by mass extermination?

And second, if the destruction of the Jews is a central element in one's ideology, a sacred task, then why conceal it? Why not proclaim it publicly, perform it publicly, relish it publicly, glory in it publicly? A profound self-contradiction lay at the very core of Nazi ideology.

There are as yet no answers to those mysteries.

Both mysteries, most especially the second, reverberate through any effort to comprehend and convey the nature of the ghetto of Theresienstadt.

What, some Nazis asked themselves, were they to do with old and sick German Jews? And the many decorated Jewish veterans of the First World War; the wounded, the amputees, the bemedaled—were they

all to be rounded up and herded off like cattle? Was that a proper way for the vaunted German Army to treat its soldiers, men who had proudly worn the uniform of Germany and fought valiantly for the Fatherland?

What of the intellectuals, the writers and composers and conductors known throughout the world, the thousands involved in film and the theater? What of spiritual leaders like Rabbi Leo Baeck?

And what of the propaganda war? How stave off possible international embarrassment if Germany's treatment of the Jews would ever become too widely known? How bring about the Final Solution and at the same time effectively conceal it from the world?

Theresienstadt was apparently conceived by Heinrich Himmler. Make Terezin a "model ghetto," exhibit it as "a town inhabited by Jews and governed by them and in which every manner of work is to be done"—Himmler's words—and solve all the awkward problems attending the Final Solution.

When the idea of such a town was broached by the Germans to the apprehensive Jewish community of Prague, it was greeted with considerable surprise and relief. Terezin would be patrolled by Czech police. There were to be no SS troops within its walls. It would be an "autonomous ghetto" run by Jews for Jews. It would even have its own currency, with a picture on the notes of Moses carrying the Ten Commandments. Small wonder the Czech Jewish community cooperated with the Germans to prepare Theresienstadt for its occupants.

The town was to take on the benign, humanitarian face the Germans at times cynically turned toward the free world. In the words of the Nazi propaganda film shot there in 1944, Theresienstadt was a gift "the Führer has given the Jews" to prepare them for life in Palestine.

The Gestapo trumpeted it in advertisements to the Jews of Germany. Admission rights were sold to privileged Jews: civil servants, members of the Jewish Councils, half-Jews, Jews married to Aryans, veterans of the First World War—all could, for a payment of tens of thousands of marks, sign the contract that would enable them to live in Theresienstadt—or so they thought.

A transport arrived in November 1941: young men assigned to prepare the camp. Then came transports of Czech Jews and more young

men. Here is an account of the early days of that ghetto by a survivor of those transports:

> The men leave for work every day in groups. They are always ac-
> companied by sentries. At the end of the first week in December, they
> are separated from the women and children, and the staff also move into
> a special building.
>
> The hopes for life in the work camp gradually disappear with the wave
> of prohibitions and orders issued daily: men are forbidden to meet to-
> gether with women; it is forbidden to write home; contact with the
> Gentile population is prohibited; smoking is punished; nobody is al-
> lowed to walk on the pavement, and every uniformed person must be
> saluted. . . .
>
> The prisoners . . . are punished by 10 to 50 blows with a small cane
> for small offenses, for larger ones by several months' imprisonment as
> well. . . .
>
> Orders of the self-governing body are issued daily, passing on the
> orders of the Nazi Command. . . . The basic organization takes shape:
> every room has its commander, several rooms together form a group.
> . . . The food commissariat is established, the technical commissariat,
> the sick bay, kitchen, central labor office, and disciplinary service. But
> there are no vehicles for transport, no equipment for the clinic, not
> enough boilers for the kitchen, there is not enough water, there is no
> fuel, there is nothing at all.

The Gentile population was evacuated and the town became entirely Jewish.

Elderly Jews, when they arrived, were often found to have brought with them their laces, parasols, top hats, and tuxedos. What they dis-covered was a town built for a population of at most 8,000 that was soon to have within its walls close to 60,000.

The words of a judge who survived:

> The new life was hardest on the old people. Many had been told in
> Germany that if they signed their property away, they would be sent to
> an old-age home. Instead they were brought here, to sleep on the floor,
> shorn of all their familiar possessions. Many of them had no close relatives
> left, and merely lived on, depressed and listless.

A dysentery epidemic broke out, and many of the older people were affected. . . . Thousands were so weak that they could not get up, and literally died in their own excrement.

For many Theresienstadt was only a transit camp. The dreaded transports would eventually take them farther east. "Transport" was a word of terror; it paralyzed all life and thinking. One heard the order "Five thousand people to be processed!" Who would be called—your friend, your mother, your child, yourself?

Odd and horrifying events occurred.

Writing letters to members of one's family outside the ghetto was a criminal act.

On January 10, 1942, the daily order announced the arrest of a group in connection with the smuggling of a letter. They were guilty under martial law.

Nine were hanged.

On February 26 of that year, seven more were hanged.

The Council of Elders, the Jewish body governing the ghetto under the direction of the SS, and under orders to be present, stood watching.

In July 1943, a transport arrived with about 1,200 Jewish children from Poland. Caked with dirt and crawling with lice, they were placed in an off-limits area. Fifty-three doctors and nurses were selected to tend to them. No one else, not even the leader of the Council of Jews, was allowed near them. Someone managed to discover that they were the remnants of the Bialystok ghetto, which had risen against the Nazis and been burned to the ground.

Six weeks later, the children were loaded onto railroad cars, together with the doctors and nurses who had cared for them. All were taken to Auschwitz, where they died.

And there was the young man who had served in the German Army and was a member of Hitler Youth. Someone discovered that his father had a Jewish grandmother. Suddenly a Jew, the young man was put on a transport to Theresienstadt.

One day a woman was brought in by two SS officers. Her four sons had lost their lives fighting for Germany. With the death of her last son, her legal standing as a privileged Jew had evaporated, and she was brought to Theresienstadt.

A man lost his Aryan wife and son in an air raid. He, too, ended up in Theresienstadt.

It was the Nazis who decided who was and who was not a Jew.

Bewildering ambiguities took place.

The Nazis had no intention of letting any of the Jews of Theresienstadt survive the war, and yet they seemed seriously concerned at times about the ghetto's appearance in the eyes of the outside world.

On June 23, 1944, a commission of the International Red Cross arrived to inspect the ghetto. Elaborate preparations were made for that inspection and for the propaganda picture that was filmed soon afterward: buildings were painted and gardens planted, invalids and poorly dressed old people were ordered off the streets, stores were filled with goods, new furniture appeared in the apartments of prominent prisoners, cultural events were planned, nurses were given clean white uniforms, lovely street signs were put up. Theresienstadt took on the look of a country resort.

The war was going poorly then for the Germans. Did they now feel it wise to attempt to convince the world that they were treating their Jews well?

The Red Cross officials looked around, asked polite questions, and seemed impressed. To this day, it is not clear if they were taken in by the ruse or reported positively on what they saw because there was little else they could do.

And was the film that was made soon afterward a typically outrageous piece of pure antisemitic Nazi propaganda? See how well the Jews are living while Europe and the Third Reich are being destroyed! Or might it have been an attempt to show the neutral countries that the Nazis had not really mistreated the Jews? Was it perhaps both, at one and the same time?

The day after the picture was completed, the noted German actor Kurt Gerron, who had played a major role in the making of the film, was sent off to Auschwitz, where he died in the gas chambers.

Auschwitz was the Kingdom of Death. Theresienstadt was the Kingdom of Deceit.

Most of the inhabitants were aware of the shriveling air of deception in which they lived. Some were more aware of it than others.

The Council of Elders ran the internal affairs of the ghetto: Jewish leaders (the Elder was appointed by the German commandant) who were responsible for a host of administrative tasks—food distribution, sanitation, cultural activities, care of the old and the young, and the lists of names for deportation.

Did the members of the council know they were sending people to certain death? We shall never know.

Deportation was the pervasive horror, yet there lingered the hope that the end was not death but useful labor that would preserve life. Had not postcards arrived from previous deportees to the "family camps" in Auschwitz extolling the merits of the place?

One man, it is reported, learned of the full horror of Auschwitz in 1943: Rabbi Leo Baeck. Bent figure, white beard, moving quietly among the people, lecturing on Plato and Kant, pulling at the garbage wagons, caring for children—Rabbi Baeck, one of the saintliest of Theresienstadt's inmates, embodied in his dignified affirmation of life the classic Jewish response to the death world of the Nazis. Upon learning the truth about the death camps, he reasoned: What would be gained by telling the truth of Auschwitz to others? Panic, despair, mass suicide. He elected to keep the truth to himself.

The ghetto—starved, sick, redolent of dread—throbbed with culture: lectures, concerts, theater. Theresienstadt was saturated with Jewish scholars, doctors, engineers, singers, diplomats, actors, composers, artists; it was a hothouse of European intellectuals. And there were 60,000 books in its library. Culture was a collective means of resisting the deceptions practiced by the Nazis as well as a weapon against despair, a way of warding off the fearful pink slip—the deportation order to the darkness in the East: "You and your family are to report at [*time and date*] at [*place*] to go on labor assignment to the East."

And the children—did they know that death lay waiting for them, too? It is probable that many of them did, in the way that children get to know things, by tunneling beneath adult deceits and repressions and coming upon truths they sense with animal keenness, truths that fuel their darkest terrors.

Petr Fischl, age fifteen, wrote:

> We got used to standing in line at seven o'clock in the morning, at twelve noon, and again at seven o'clock in the evening. We stood in a long queue with a plate in our hand, into which they ladled a little warmed-up water with a salty or a coffee flavor. . . . We got used to sleeping without a bed. . . . We got used to undeserved slaps, blows, and executions. We got accustomed to seeing people die in their own

excrement, to seeing piled-up coffins full of corpses, to seeing the sick amid dirt and filth and to seeing the helpless doctors.

Petr Fischl died in Auschwitz in 1944.

Children also wrote poetry, of which Pavel Friedmann's "The Butterfly," written in June 1942, is probably the best known:

> For seven weeks I've lived in here,
> Penned up inside this ghetto.
> But I have found what I love here.
> The dandelions call to me
> And the white chestnut branches in the court.
> Only I never saw another butterfly.
>
> That butterfly was the last one.
> Butterflies don't live in here,
>   In the ghetto.

What did it do to those children, that ghetto, the sunlight of the day and the terrors of the night, their dreamy remembrances of the past and their desolate encounters with the present? Much of what it did to them we can see in the art they left behind.

In Theresienstadt there were art classes taught by well-known artists. One of those artists was a quite remarkable figure: Friedl Dicker-Brandeis.

Vienna-born, Bauhaus-trained; a secularist, a Communist, a painter of portraits and landscapes; an émigré to Prague and later a Czech citizen; an active anti-Fascist who, because she felt her place was in Europe, turned down a visa that would have enabled her to enter Palestine—Friedl Dicker-Brandeis became, in December 1942, a resident of Theresienstadt.

People describe her as small, fragile, patient; a short haircut, large expressive eyes. Her tastes were highly sophisticated, and she managed somehow, under those terrible conditions, to make a livable space out of the tiny under-the-staircase closet she occupied. Others who taught expected and received compensation in bread; she would accept no payment for her teaching. She would go from group to group, calmly

and instinctively teaching, though she had no pedagogical education. The children waited for her quietly, eagerly. She did not know Czech and spoke only German, yet that didn't seem to matter. She taught in the way she herself had been taught by her art teachers in Vienna and the Bauhaus: exercises in breathing and rhythm; the study of reproductions, texture, color values; the importance of observation, patience; the freeing of oneself from the outer world of numbing routine and the inner world of dread. She would tell stories, and the children would be required to draw the objects she had mentioned twice. They drew flowers, butterflies, animals, cities, storms, rainbows, streets, railway stations, family portraits, holidays, merry-go-rounds. They drew their concealed inner worlds, their tortured emotions, which Friedl Dicker-Brandeis was then able to enter and try to heal. She helped restore a balance to the trembling consciousness of terrified children.

The children of Theresienstadt created about 5,000 drawings and collages. Friedl Dicker-Brandeis herself drew very little—she saved the paper and paint for the children.

A member of those classes who survived said of her: "I remember Mrs. Brandeis as a tender, highly intelligent woman, who managed— for some hours every week—to create a fairy world for us in Terezin . . . a world that made us forget all the surrounding hardships, which we were not spared despite our early age."

Friedl Dicker-Brandeis was deported to Auschwitz on October 6, 1944, and died in Birkenau.

Nazi Germany lost the war against the Western democracies and the Soviet Union and won the war against the Jews.

The Germans destroyed 80 percent of European Jewry.

Jewish self-perception—indeed, all of humankind's understanding of reality and human nature, human destiny, the way we think about the world—all have been forever altered.

The statistics of Theresienstadt, cold and numbing, each digit a human being:

As of April 20, 1945, there arrived from Germany, Holland, Denmark, Poland, Luxembourg, Austria, Hungary, Czechoslovakia, and a few other places, a little over 141,000 Jews.

• 33,456 died in the ghetto.
• 88,202 were transported to the death camps in the East.

On May 9, 1945, there remained in Theresienstadt a total of 16,832 Jews.

Of the 15,000 children deported from Theresienstadt to Auschwitz, 100 survived—none under the age of fourteen.

Statistics.

Theresienstadt was liberated by the Soviet Army on May 8, 1945.

Willy Groag, a former prisoner of Terezin and today a chemist, artist, and member of an Israeli kibbutz, was appointed coordinator of the children and youth department of the ghetto at the war's end. His responsibility was the rapid repatriation of the ghetto's young population.

One day in late August 1945, he was entrusted by Raja Engländerová, a former student of Friedl Dicker-Brandeis, with two suitcases of children's drawings. He brought the suitcases to the Prague Jewish community. The authorities there evinced little interest in them. For ten years the suitcases sat on a shelf, collecting dust.

Then the drawings were rediscovered and exhibited. They have since been seen by millions throughout the world.

Many of those drawings, as well as poems, by the children of Theresienstadt are in this volume.

The last remaining Jews left Theresienstadt on August 17, 1945.

Terezin has since returned to its tranquil surroundings. Virtually no trace remains of those nightmarish ghetto years. One sees the rolling hills, the gentle juncture of the two rivers, the Bohemian mountains. And butterflies.

. . . only I never saw another butterfly . . .

AT TEREZIN

When a new child comes
Everything seems strange to him.
What, on the ground I have to lie?
Eat black potatoes? No! Not I!
I've got to stay? It's dirty here!
The floor—why, look, it's dirt, I fear!
And I'm supposed to sleep on it?
I'll get all dirty!

Here the sound of shouting, cries,
And oh, so many flies.
Everyone knows flies carry disease.
Oooh, something bit me! Wasn't that a bedbug?
Here in Terezin, life is hell
And when I'll go home again, I can't yet tell.

Teddy
L 410, 1943

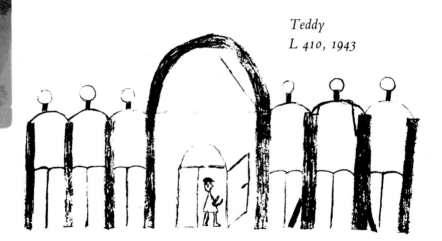

THE CLOSED TOWN

Everything leans, like tottering, hunched old women.

Every eye shines with fixed waiting
and for the word "when?"

Here there are few soldiers.
Only the shot-down birds tell of war.

You believe every bit of news you hear.

The buildings now are fuller,
Body smelling close to body,
And the garrets scream with light for long, long hours.

This evening I walked along the street of death.
On one wagon, they were taking the dead away.

Why so many marches have been drummed here?

Why so many soldiers?

Then
A week after the end,
Everything will be empty here.
A hungry dove will peck for bread.
In the middle of the street will stand
An empty, dirty
Hearse.

Anonymous

We got used to standing in line at seven o'clock in the morning, at twelve noon, and again at seven o'clock in the evening. We stood in a long queue with a plate in our hand, into which they ladled a little warmed-up water with a salty or a coffee flavor. Or else they gave us a few potatoes. We got used to sleeping without a bed, to saluting every uniform, not to walk on the sidewalks and then again to walk on the sidewalks. We got used to undeserved slaps, blows, and executions. We got accustomed to seeing people die in their own excrement, to seeing piled-up coffins full of corpses, to seeing the sick amid dirt and filth and to seeing the helpless doctors. We got used to it that from time to time, one thousand unhappy souls would come here and that, from time to time, another thousand unhappy souls would go away. . . .

From the prose of fifteen-year-old Petr Fischl (born September 9, 1929),
who perished in Auschwitz in 1944

Kitty Passow a
27 . 3 hod

THE OLD HOUSE

Deserted here, the old house
stands in silence, asleep.
The old house used to be so nice,
before, standing there,
it was so nice.
Now it is deserted,
rotting in silence—
What a waste of houses,
a waste of hours.

Franta Bass

HOME

I look, I look
into the wide world,
into the wide, distant world.
I look to the southeast,
I look, I look toward my home.

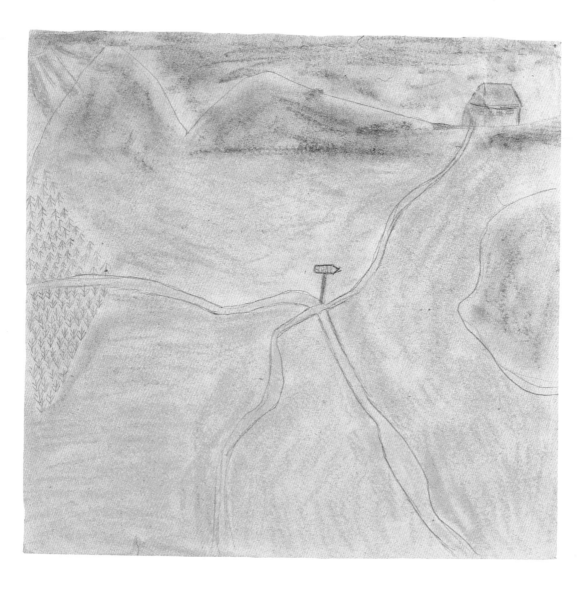

I look toward my home,
the city where I was born.
City, my city,
I will gladly return to you.

Franta Bass

IT ALL DEPENDS ON HOW YOU LOOK AT IT

I.

Terezin is full of beauty.
It's in your eyes now clear
And through the street the tramp
Of many marching feet I hear.

In the ghetto at Terezin,
It looks that way to me,
Is a square kilometer of earth
Cut off from the world that's free.

II.

Death, after all, claims everyone,
You find it everywhere.
It catches up with even those
Who wear their noses in the air.

The whole, wide world is ruled
With a certain justice, so
That helps perhaps to sweeten
The poor man's pain and woe.

Miroslav Košek

MAN PROPOSES, GOD DISPOSES

I.

Who was helpless back in Prague,
And who was rich before,
He's a poor soul here in Terezin,
His body's bruised and sore.

II.

Who was toughened up before,
He'll survive these days.
But who was used to servants
Will sink into his grave.

Koleba (Miroslav Košek, Hanuš Löwy,
Bachner)
26. II. 1944

TEREZIN

The heaviest wheel rolls across our foreheads
To bury itself deep somewhere inside our memories.

We've suffered here more than enough,
Here in this clot of grief and shame,
Wanting a badge of blindness
To be a proof for their own children.

A fourth year of waiting, like standing above a swamp
From which any moment might gush forth a spring.

Meanwhile, the rivers flow another way,
Another way,
Not letting you die, not letting you live.

And the cannons don't scream and the guns don't bark
And you don't see blood here.
Nothing, only silent hunger.
Children steal the bread here and ask and ask
            and ask
And all would wish to sleep, keep silent, and
    just to go to sleep again . . .

The heaviest wheel rolls across our foreheads
To bury itself deep somewhere inside our memories.

Mif 1944

TEREZIN

That bit of filth in dirty walls,
And all around barbed wire,
And 30,000 souls who sleep
Who once will wake
And once will see
Their own blood spilled.

I was once a little child,
Three years ago,
That child who longed for other worlds.
But now I am no more a child
For I have learned to hate.
I am a grown-up person now,
I have known fear.

Bloody words and a dead day then,
That's something different than bogeymen!

But anyway, I still believe I only sleep today,
That I'll wake up, a child again, and start to laugh and play.
I'll go back to childhood sweet like a briar rose,
Like a bell that wakes us from a dream,
Like a mother with an ailing child
Loves him with aching woman's love.
How tragic, then, is youth that lives
With enemies, with gallows ropes,
How tragic, then, for children on your lap
To say: this for the good, that for the bad.

Somewhere, far away out there, childhood sweetly sleeps,
Along that path among the trees,
There o'er that house
That was once my pride and joy.
There my mother gave me birth into this world
So I could weep . . .

In the flame of candles by my bed, I sleep
And once perhaps I'll understand
That I was such a little thing,
As little as this song.

These 30,000 souls who sleep
Among the trees will wake,
Open an eye
And because they see
A lot

They'll fall asleep again . . .

Hanuš Hachenburg
IX. 1944

LIGHTS OUT

. . . Three young boys ran away. For that we have already had a week of "confinement to barracks" and "lights out." We walk only in columns to work, and after six o'clock in the evening, no one is allowed on the street. We come home from work in the dark and in the morning we go to work in the dark. We dress and undress by the touch system. Our windows must be darkened and it is forbidden to have any sort of light. Tomorrow I'm going to the Hamburg barracks for bread and perhaps I'll manage to see Mom. . . .

"Confinement" has been canceled, but "lights out" continues, evidently for the whole winter. We have to save on electricity. Each of the different blocks gets it every third day in turn. We may use candles for light, but they don't last long. Supplies from home are being used up and we can't manage to get more. It is terribly stupid, we can't even read in the evening. Without light everything is so sad and gloomy. I am awfully homesick for Prague. Evening after evening Franka and I recall things in Prague far into the night and often we dream of it in our sleep. . . .

Last night I had a beautiful dream. I dreamed that I was at home, I saw quite clearly our flat and street. Now I am disappointed and out of sorts, because I awoke in the bunk instead of my own bed. But maybe this was some sort of omen of an early end. Then there should be permanent "lights out" all over Germany. . . .

Old people's transport. Ten thousand sick, crippled, dying, all of them over sixty-five years old.

It's horrible everywhere. The rays of sun fall exactly on my bunk and reach on farther, I try in vain to get away from them into the shade. Today I shan't go and report for "Service." I haven't left out a day yet, but I am too exhausted to stand the sight of misery and suffering again. The old people's transport, the young people cannot volunteer. Children have to let their old parents go off and can't help them. Why do they want to send these defenseless people away? If they want to

get rid of us young people, I can understand that, maybe they are afraid of us, don't want us to give birth to any more Jewish children. But how can these old people be dangerous? If they had to come here to Terezin, isn't that enough, can't they let them die in peace here? After all, these old people can't hope for anything else. . . .

The barracks by the physical culture hall must be cleared out, a special dinner is being cooked, and the reception center is getting ready. They say some Polish children are coming. This is all incomprehensible. Why, and how does it happen that they are brought here from Poland?

They came yesterday at five o'clock. No one is allowed near them. In the night they called some nurses, guards, and doctors. Besides these no one is allowed near their barracks. . . . You can see them a little from the fortress wall, and then they went in the morning to the reception center. . . . They are all barelegged and only a very few have shoes. They returned from the reception center with their heads shaved, they have lice. They all have such frightened eyes. . . .

Yesterday they were taken off, doctors, nurses, and guards with them. . . .

Where they came from we never found out, nor where they were taken either. Rumors were circulating about deportation to Palestine, but no one believes this. They have gone. All that is left is a few lines scribbled on the wall of the barracks that hardly anyone can figure out.

From the diary of
Helga Weissová

MEITNER EVA

YES, THAT'S THE WAY THINGS ARE

I.

In Terezin in the so-called park
A queer old granddad sits
Somewhere there in the so-called park.
He wears a beard down to his lap
And on his head, a little cap.

II.

Hard crusts he crumbles in his gums,
He's only got one single tooth.
My poor old man with working gums,
Instead of soft rolls, lentil soup.
My poor old graybeard!

Koleba (M. Košek, H. Löwy, Bachner)

PAIN STRIKES SPARKS ON ME,
THE PAIN OF TEREZIN

Fifteen beds. Fifteen charts with names,
Fifteen people without a family tree.
Fifteen bodies for whom torture is medicine and pills,
Beds over which the crimson blood of ages spills.
Fifteen bodies that want to live here.
Thirty eyes seeking quietness.
Bald heads that gape from out of the prison.
The holiness of the suffering, which is none of my business.

The loveliness of air, which day after day
Smells of strangeness and carbolic,
The nurses that carry thermometers
Mothers who grope after a smile.
Food is such a luxury here.
A long, long night, and a brief day.

But anyway, I don't want to leave
The lighted rooms and the burning cheeks,
Nurses who leave behind them only a shadow
To help the little sufferers.

I'd like to stay here, a small patient,
Waiting the doctor's daily round,
Until, after a long, long time, I'd be well again.

Then I'd like to live
And go back home again.

Anonymous

ILLNESS

Sadness, stillness in the room.
In the middle, a table and a bed.
In the bed, a feverish boy.
His mother sits next to him
with a little book.
She reads him his favorite story
and immediately, the fever subsides.

Franta Bass

THERESIENSTADT'S HOSPITAL

Once, happier people lived here
in the gray building.
Now, death moves silently toward those other creatures,
those with typhoid, who moan and writhe
in their own diarrhea,
who lie here and don't understand
why they are being fed bread and margarine.
I enter and become silent.

"You shiny new doorknobs,
you pretty painted walls in the bright ward,
can you make up for the stench of excrement?
Can you appease the hunger
of those who are ashamed of their underwear,
and brought here to die,
day by day?"

The paint looks at me
and doesn't answer.
"Why? I don't understand why!"
It seems the doorknob would say,
when it opened for me,
a free soul, with a full stomach,
"I can tell you
and then you will come to me!"

Anonymous

CONCERT IN THE OLD SCHOOL GARRET
(played by Gideon Klein)

White fingers of the sexton sleep heavy upon us.
Half a century
Since anyone as much as touched this piano.
Let it sing again
As it was made to yesterday.

Phantom hands that strike softly or that thunder.
The forehead of this man heavy as the
      heavens before it rains.

And the springs,
Under the weight of excitement, forgot to squeak.
Half a century it is since anyone as much as touched
      this piano.

Our good friend Time
Sucked each figure empty like a honeybee
That has lived long enough
And drunk enough honey
So that now it can dry out in the sun somewhere.

Under the closed eyes, another person sits,
Under the closed eyes, he seeks among the keys
As among the veins through which the blood flows softly
When you kiss them with a knife and put a song to it.

And this man yesterday cut all the veins,
Opening all the organ's stops,
Paid all the birds to sing,
To sing

Even though the harsh fingers of the sexton
      sleep heavy upon us.
Bent in his manner of death, you are like Beethoven

Your forehead was as heavy as the heavens before it rains.

Anonymous

34

A LETTER TO DADDY

Momma told me to write to you today,
but I had no time. New children arrived
with the latest transport, and
I had to play with them.
I didn't notice time pass.

I live better these days.
I sleep on my own mattress on the floor,
so I will not fall down.
At least I don't have much work to fix up my bed,
and in the morning I see the sky from my window.

I was coughing a bit, but I don't want to get sick,
for I am happy when I can run in the courtyard.
Tonight there will be a gathering
like the ones at Scout camp in the summer.

We will sing songs we know,
a girl will play the accordion.
I know you wonder how we fare here,
and you would surely like to be with us now.

And something else, Daddy. Come soon
and have a more cheerful face!
When you are unhappy, Momma is sad,
and then I miss the sparkle in her eyes.

You promised to bring me books
because, truly, I have nothing to read.
So please, come tomorrow, right before dusk.
I will surely be grateful for this.

Now I must stop. Momma sends you her love.
I will rejoice when I hear your footsteps
in the hall. Until you are with us again,
I send you my greetings and kisses.

                              Your faithful son.

                              Anonymous

THE BUTTERFLY

The last, the very last,
So richly, brightly, dazzlingly yellow.
Perhaps if the sun's tears would sing
    against a white stone. . . .

Such, such a yellow ·
Is carried lightly 'way up high.
It went away I'm sure because it wished to
    kiss the world good-bye.

For seven weeks I've lived in here,
Penned up inside this ghetto.
But I have found what I love here.
The dandelions call to me
And the white chestnut branches in the court.
Only I never saw another butterfly.

That butterfly was the last one.
Butterflies don't live in here,
    in the ghetto.

4. 6. 1942 Pavel Friedmann

THE LITTLE MOUSE

A mousie sat upon a shelf,
Catching fleas in his coat of fur.
But he couldn't catch her—what chagrin!—
She'd hidden 'way inside his skin.
He turned and wriggled, knew no rest,
That flea was such a nasty pest!

His daddy came
And searched his coat.
He caught the flea and off he ran
To cook her in the frying pan.
The little mouse cried, "Come and see!
For lunch we've got a nice, fat flea!"

26. II. 1944 Koleba (M. Košek, H. Löwy,
Bachner)

AN EVENING IN TEREZIN

The sun goes down
and everything is silent,
only at the guard's post
are heavy footfalls heard.

That's the guard who watches his Jews
to make sure they don't run away from the ghetto,
or that an Aryan aunt or uncle
doesn't try to get in.

Ten o'clock strikes suddenly,
and the windows of Dresden's barracks darken.
The women have a lot to talk about;
they remember their homes,
and dinners they made.

Then some of them argue.
Others try to quiet them down.
Finally, one by one, they grow silent;
they toss and turn, and in the end,
they fall asleep.

How many more evenings
will we have to live like this?
We do not know,
only God knows.

Eva Schulzová

VII. 1944

HOMESICK

I've lived in the ghetto here for more than a
   year,
In Terezin, in the black town now,
And when I remember my old home so dear,
I can love it more than I did, somehow.

Ah, home, home,
Why did they tear me away?
Here the weak die easy as a feather
And when they die, they die forever.

I'd like to go back home again,
It makes me think of sweet spring flowers.
Before, when I used to live at home,
It never seemed so dear and fair.

I remember now those golden days . . .
But maybe I'll be going there soon again.

People walk along the street,
You see at once on each you meet
That there's ghetto here,
A place of evil and of fear.
There's little to eat and much to want,
Where bit by bit, it's horror to live.
But no one must give up!
The world turns and times change.

Yet we all hope the time will come
When we'll go home again.
Now I know how dear it is
And often I remember it.

9. III. 1943 *Anonymous*

Doris Weiser

I'D LIKE TO GO ALONE

I'd like to go away alone
Where there are other, nicer people,
Somewhere into the far unknown,
There, where no one kills another.

Maybe more of us,
A thousand strong,
Will reach this goal
Before too long.

Alena Synková

NIGHT IN THE GHETTO

Another day has gone for keeps
Into the bottomless pit of time.
Again it has wounded a man, held captive
    by his brethren.
After dusk, he longs for bandages,
For soft hands to shield the eyes
From all the horrors that stare by day.
But in the ghetto, darkness, too, is kind
To weary eyes that all day long
    have had to watch.

Dawn crawls again along the ghetto streets
Embracing all who walk this way.
Only a car like a greeting from a long-gone world
Gobbles up the dark with fiery eyes—
That sweet darkness that falls upon the soul
And heals those wounds illumined by the day . . .
Along the streets come light and ranks of people
Like a long black ribbon, loomed with gold.

1943 Anonymous

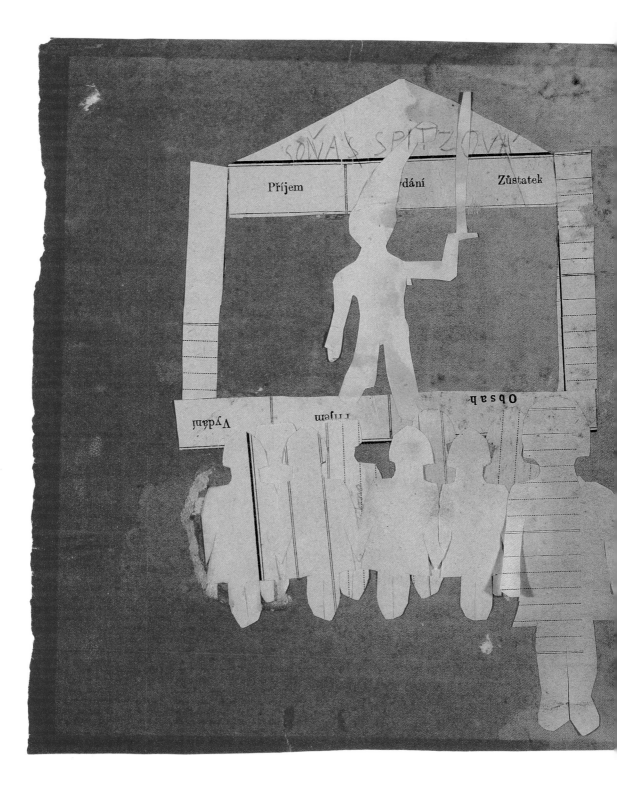

FEAR

Today the ghetto knows a different fear,
Close in its grip, Death wields an icy scythe.
An evil sickness spreads a terror in its wake,
The victims of its shadow. weep and writhe.

Today a father's heartbeat tells his fright
And mothers bend their heads into their hands.
Now children choke and die with typhus here,
A bitter tax is taken from their bands.

My heart still beats inside my breast
While friends depart for other worlds.
Perhaps it's better—who can say?—
Than watching this, to die today?

No, no, my God, we want to live!
Not watch our numbers melt away.
We want to have a better world,
We want to work—we must not die!

Eva Picková, 12 years old, Nymburk

I AM A JEW

I am a Jew and will be a Jew forever.
Even if I should die from hunger,
never will I submit.
I will always fight for my people,
on my honor.
I will never be ashamed of them,
I give my word.

I am proud of my people,
how dignified they are.
Even though I am suppressed,
I will always come back to life.

Franta Bass

DUSK

The dusk flew in on the wings of evening . . .
From whom do you bring me a greeting?
Will you kiss my lips for him?
How I long for the place where I was born!

Perhaps only you, tranquil dusk,
know of the tears shed in your lap
from eyes that long to see
the shade of palms and olive trees
in the land of Israel.

Perhaps only you will understand
this daughter of Zion,
who weeps
for her small city on the Elbe★
but is afraid ever to return to it.

Anonymous

★ The Elbe is a river that flows from Germany to Czechoslovakia.

TO OLGA

Listen!
The boat whistle has sounded now
And we must sail
Out toward an unknown port.

We'll sail a long, long way
And dreams will turn to truth.
Oh, how sweet the name Morocco!
Listen!
Now it's time.

The wind sings songs of far away,
Just look up to heaven
And think about the violets.

Listen!
Now it's time.

Alena Synková

. . . The commission, because of which a transport left and the three-layer bunks were torn down, has departed, and I believe they were satisfied. They didn't see through very much, stayed scarcely a half day, but that seems to have been only a rehearsal. The camp command issued new orders about the "beautifying campaign" that must be finished in two months.

It's ridiculous, but it seems that Terezin is to be changed into a sort of spa. I don't know why I was reminded of the fairy tale "Table, Set Yourself!" But that is how everything seems to me. The orders are received in the evening, and in the morning everyone's eyes are staring with wonder, where did this or that thing come from? For three years it never occurred to anyone that streets might be named anything but Q and L. . . . But all of a sudden the Germans had an idea, and overnight signs had to be put on every corner house with the name of the street, and at crossroads arrows pointed: To the Park, To the Bath, etc. . . .

The school building that had served as hospital up to today was cleared out overnight and the patients put elsewhere while the whole building was repainted, scrubbed up, school benches brought in, and in the morning a sign could be seen afar: "Boys' and Girls' School." It really looks fine, like a real school, only the pupils and teachers are missing. That shortcoming is adjusted by a small note on the door: "Holidays." On the square the newly sown grass is coming up, the center is adorned by a big rose plot, and the paths, covered with clean, yellow sand, are lined with two rows of newly painted benches. The boards we wondered about for so many days, trying to puzzle out what they were for, turned into a music pavilion. We even have a café with the fine sign "Coffeehouse."

. . . They have already got quite far in painting the houses. . . . In two of the barracks some bunks and shelves were painted yellow and they got blue curtains. In the park in front of the Infants' Home they put up a luxury pavilion with cribs and light blue, quilted covers. In one room there are toys, a carved rocking horse, and so on. None of us can explain why they are doing all this. Are they so concerned about that commission? Perhaps we don't even know how good the situation is.

From the diary of Helga Weissová

FORGOTTEN

You wanton, quiet memory that haunts me all the while
In order to remind me of her whom love I send.
Perhaps when you caress me sweetly, I will smile,
You are my confidante today, my very dearest friend.

You sweet remembrance, tell a fairy tale
About my girl who's lost and gone, you see.
Tell, tell the one about the golden grail
And call the swallow, bring her back to me.

Fly somewhere back to her and ask her, soft and low,
If she thinks of me sometimes with love,
If she is well and ask her, too, before you go
If I am still her dearest, precious dove.

And hurry back, don't lose your way,
So I can think of other things,
But you were too lovely, perhaps, to stay.
I loved you once. Good-bye, my love!

Anonymous

CAMPFIRE (to Eva Landová)

Here I sit on a rock
in front of the campfire.
One branch after another
is snatched by the fire.
Into the darkness
the forest recedes.

Fire makes one reflect . . .
Terezin is all I think about.
But now memories gather 'round me
like the falling leaves.

Fall is here.
The leaves turn yellow on the trees,
the campfire dies out.
My thoughts are far from here,
somewhere far,
where integrity lives.

It lives in my friend.
Now I think of her.
Memories gather 'round me
like the falling leaves.

                    A. Lindtová

UNTITLED

I've met enough people.
Seldom a human being.
Therefore, I will wait—
until my life's purpose
is fulfilled
and you will come.

Though there is anguish
deep in my soul—
what if I must search for you forever?—
I must not lose faith,
I must not lose hope.

Alena Synková

THE GARDEN

A little garden,
Fragrant and full of roses.
The path is narrow
And a little boy walks along it.

A little boy, a sweet boy,
Like that growing blossom.
When the blossom comes to bloom,
The little boy will be no more.

Franta Bass

zakázané ovoce.

TEARS

And thereafter come . . .
tears,
without them
there is no life.
Tears—
inspired by grief
tears
that fall like rain.

Alena Synková

caja 25

ON A SUNNY EVENING

On a purple, sun-shot evening
Under wide-flowering chestnut trees
Upon the threshold full of dust
Yesterday, today, the days are all like these.

Trees flower forth in beauty,
Lovely, too, their very wood all gnarled and old
That I am half afraid to peer
Into their crowns of green and gold.

The sun has made a veil of gold
So lovely that my body aches.
Above, the heavens shriek with blue
Convinced I've smiled by some mistake.
The world's abloom and seems to smile.
I want to fly but where, how high?
If in barbed wire, things can bloom
Why couldn't I? I will not die!

1944 Anonymous
Written by the children in Barracks L318 and
L417, ages 10–16 years.

THE STORM

The heavens sense our burden:
the threat of future downpours
I carry on my back.
We are drunk on wine vinegar.
The nearing storm rouses me,
it makes me want to shake the world.

We are an assembly of misery.
If our hands are bloody,
it is from the blood of our own wounds.
The grotesque scars
we bear on our bodies
testify to battles fought
that went unrecognized.

But the next storm will unfurl our flag
and uproot the rotted trees!
Then we, together with the gusting wind,
will scale Spilberk's★ heights,
and stand in victory on the peaks of cliffs,
our hair blowing freely in the wind.

Jirka Polak

★ Spilberk was a famous jail in the Middle Ages in the city of Brno.

BIRDSONG

He doesn't know the world at all
Who stays in his nest and doesn't go out.
He doesn't know what birds know best
Nor what I want to sing about,
That the world is full of loveliness.

When dewdrops sparkle in the grass
And earth's aflood with morning light,
A blackbird sings upon a bush
To greet the dawning after night.
Then I know how fine it is to live.

Hey, try to open up your heart
To beauty; go to the woods someday
And weave a wreath of memory there.
Then if the tears obscure your way
You'll know how wonderful it is
        To be alive.

1941 Anonymous

BIRDSONG II

The poor thing stands there vainly,
Vainly he strains his voice.
Perhaps he'll die. Then can you say
How beautiful is the world today?

Anonymous

The children's drawings from Terezin collected in this publication have been chosen from a total of 4,000 drawings in the archives of the State Jewish Museum in Prague. They were given to the museum during the postwar collection of documents on the persecution at Terezin. The drawings were given in envelopes bearing the number of different "homes" (e.g., CIII, BIV, 1417, etc.) where the children lived at Terezin and where they were secretly given schooling.

To illustrate this publication, two kinds of drawings were chosen: some as illustrations of the poems' texts, others for their artistic value. A total of 53 children are represented in the illustrations. The dates of their birth and death are listed, if known. From indications on the drawings themselves and a comparison of the children's biographical material, it has been established that the earliest drawing dates from 1943, although it is known that the children were drawing pictures as soon as they came to Terezin.

Children were consciously guided to drawing, as is indicated by the notes of the instructors who taught in the girls' and boys' dormitories. The teaching program was carefully planned and classes were divided into several levels. They began with the required fundamentals of drawing (wavy lines, circles), and later the children drew pictures of everyday objects they saw around them at Terezin, such as jelly jars filled with meadow flowers, and finally complicated still lifes, drawn from nature.

From the artistic standpoint, the most interesting are the collages, made out of all sorts of materials that happened to be around, such as old office forms, wrapping paper, etc., and that were cut or torn into various shapes and designs.

The great majority of the drawings date from the first half of 1944. Fewer are found from the autumn of 1944, when the steady shipment of Terezin prisoners eastward, toward Auschwitz, interrupted the school program and when the majority of the children, together with their drawing teacher, Friedl Dicker-Brandeis, left Terezin.

Page i **MAN HOLDING NEWSPAPER WITH AN INCORRECTLY WRITTEN INSCRIPTION, TAGESBEHFEL (official Terezin bulletin)**
The detail of the upper right part of the drawing "Scenes from Life at Terezin," a drawing on both sides of the paper, done in pencil and pastel crayon on semiglossy yellow paper (archive number 129075, 1942–1945 written in later). On the other side of the drawing, "Zuzka Winterová Block IV 4/8" is written in the upper right corner.
Zuzana Winterová was born on January 27, 1933, in Brno, and deported to Terezin on April 4, 1942. She is represented in the collection of children's drawings from Terezin by another pastel, "Mommy with a Baby Carriage," dated April 11, 1944, and the sketch "Elephant," from April 18, 1944, which was a common assignment for children in her age group who were living in Block IV. She perished in Auschwitz on October 4, 1944.

Page ii **BIRD AND BUTTERFLY**

A paper collage with watercolor and pencil (archive number 129765). The artist is unknown.

Page iii **BUTTERFLY**

Detail from middle of drawing "Butterflies," a pencil and pastel sketch on the back of a piece of semiglossy yellow paper (archive number 129979). Signed in upper right corner "Marika Friedmanová Heim 13 skupina IV".

Marika Friedmanová was born on April 19, 1933, and deported to Terezin on August 3, 1942. There are 23 more of her drawings included in the collection. One of them was dated May 10 (1944). She lived in building L410, house 13. She perished in Auschwitz in 1944.

Page v **FLOWERS IN JAR**

Detail from a watercolor and pencil sketch done on both sides of a piece of drawing paper (archive number 129.940). Signed "4 h Erika Taussig."

For biographical note see catalog entry for p. 31.

Page vi **BUTTERFLIES**

A pencil drawing on the back of a double sheet of glossy yellow paper (archive number 129498). On the front, "Eva Bu" (Bulová) is written in the upper right corner.

Eva Bulová was born on July 12, 1930, at Řevnice near Prague and brought to Terezin on September 12, 1942. She is represented by 11 other drawings in this collection, the most interesting of which artistically is the collage "Portrait of a Woman with Long Hair." At Terezin Eva lived in house number 28 and was put into Group A. She died October 4, 1944, at Auschwitz. See also p. xxii.

Page ix **VIEW OF TEREZIN**

Detail from a crayon drawing (archive number 121991) signed in pencil "Weidmann Petr, 2 V 1944, 13½," in upper left corner.

Complete drawing by Petr Weidmann on p. 12; biographical note of catalog entry for p. 12.

Page x **SKETCH OF CHILD'S HAND**

The reverse side of a pencil sketch (archive number 129411). In the lower right corner of the other side is written "František Brozan L 417 Heim X 2."

František Brozan was born on December 13, 1932, in Staňkov and deported to Terezin on November 30, 1942. He is represented in this collection by two more drawings: a pencil sketch, "Tools," which was an assignment for children of his age, and a watercolor, "Landscape." He lived in house number 10 at Terezin and died at Auschwitz on December 15, 1943.

Page xxi **BUTTERFLIES**

A detail from "Butterflies" (archive number 129979) by Marika Friedmanová. For biographical note see catalog entry for p. iii.

from Prague on July 16, 1942. He was transported to Auschwitz on October 12, 1944, where he perished.

Pages **QUEUE FOR FOOD**
6–7 Detail from a drawing entitled "Serving Meals," which covers both sides of a piece of wrapping paper and is drawn in pencil (archive number 129204). Written on the reverse is "Liana Franklová HOD. 13, DOMOV 13."

Liana Franklová was born in Brno on January 12, 1931, and deported to Terezin on December 5, 1941. Another 19 of her drawings are included in the collection, most of them pastels and watercolors, dating between March and May 1944. In Terezin she lived in house 13 and belonged to Group IV. She died in Auschwitz on October 19, 1944.

Page 8 **FLOWERS IN VASE**
Collage of cut paper and office ledger paper painted over with tempera (archive number 133573), signed "Kitty Passerová 27.3.nod" in lower left corner.

Kitty Markéta Passerová was born on September 4, 1929, and deported to Terezin from Prague on December 8, 1943. She was liberated from Terezin in May 1945. Kitty Hest lives today in Bondi Junction, Australia.

Page 9 **HOUSE**
A pasted collage on an office form (archive number 129715). Signature on reverse side: "Valentíková Dita I. s."

Dita Valentíková was born in 1933, but nothing more is known about her. There are 15 more drawings by her in the collection, dated from May and June 1944. In Terezin she lived in building L410, house 16, and in building CIII. She belonged to Group I.

Page 10 **HOUSE AT TEREZIN**
Watercolor on shiny paper (archive number 129917), no signature.

Hana Kohnová was born on July 7, 1931, and deported to Terezin from Prague on December 14, 1941. She was sent to Auschwitz on May 18, 1944, where she perished.

Page 11 **FARAWAY HOUSE**
Pastel and pencil on paper (archive number 129319).

Hana Erika Karplusová was born on January 4, 1930, and arrived at Terezin on April 4, 1942. She was a student of Friedl Dicker-Brandeis. She was sent to Auschwitz on October 6, 1944, where she perished.

Page 12 **VIEW OF TEREZIN**
A crayon drawing (archive number 121991) signed in pencil "Weidmann Petr, 2 V 1944, 13 1/2," in upper left corner.

Petr Weidmann was born on September 1, 1930. He was deported to Terezin from Prague on November 20, 1942. He was sent to Auschwitz on October 4, 1944, where he perished.

Pages **FIGURE WITH BANDAGE AND CARICATURE OF A MAN**
14–15 Details from a sketch, "The Ailing." It is a pencil drawing on tinted paper
(bot- (archive number 129205). No signature.
tom)

Page 15 VIEW OF TEREZIN

A paper collage (archive number 131296). On the other side of the paper is written "Hans Weinberg HEIM II stunde 6."

Hanuš Weinberg was born in Ústí nad Orlicí on August 18, 1931, and deported to Terezin on December 5, 1942. Two more of his watercolors and two pencil sketches, their themes suggested by his teacher, are included in the collection. In Terezin he lived in boys' dormitory II. He perished in Auschwitz on December 15, 1943.

Page 16 LABOR BRIGADES

A pencil drawing (archive number 133502) signed "Novák. J. x 13 had" at lower right.

Josef Novák was born on October 25, 1931, in Prague and deported to Terezin on April 24, 1942. Another 16 sketches, watercolors, and pencil drawings have been preserved in the collection of children's art from Terezin. (See also p. 47.) The subject matter of the drawings dated 1943 have a patriotic inspiration ("Flowering of the Czech Nation," "For the Nation"), but there is also a picture of a Terezin execution (January 1, 1942), made from a description he had heard. He lived in boys' dormitory X in Terezin and was a student of Friedl Dicker-Brandeis. He was deported to Auschwitz and died on May 18, 1944.

Pages **TEREZIN**
18–19 A collage using office paper pasted on shiny yellow paper (archive number 129738) signed "Ruth [illegible]" in upper right corner.

Ruth Schachterová was born on August 24, 1930. She was deported to Terezin from Brno on March 19, 1942. She was a student of Friedl Dicker-Brandeis. She was sent to Auschwitz on May 18, 1944, where she perished.

Page 21 NAZI THREATENING JEW

A pencil drawing on paper (archive number 125426), signed on back "Beutler, Jiri 2 32."

Jiri Beutler was born on August 9, 1932. He was deported to Terezin on September 18, 1942, and was sent to Auschwitz on May 18, 1944, where he died.

Page 23 CHECKING FOR LICE

An ink and watercolor drawing (archive number 131978) signed in lower right corner "Helga Weissová heim 24."

Helga Weissová was born in Prague on November 10, 1929. She was deported to Terezin at age 12 with her mother and father. Too old to par-

ticipate in the children's drawing classes, she drew independently and also illustrated a book written by her father, *God Came to Terezin and Saw That It Was Bad.* In October 1944 she was sent to Auschwitz and on to work camps; she and her mother survived the war and returned to Prague. After the war she studied art with Emil Filla. Helga Weissová-Hošková lives and is an artist in Prague. (See diary excerpts on pp. 22, 24, and 62.)

Page 25 DEPORTATION TRAIN

Detail from a pencil drawing (archive number 133381). The artist's signature is incorporated into the flowing waters of a river, "III Holzbauer."

Petr Holzbauer was born on January 29, 1932, and deported to Terezin from Prague on December 22, 1942. He was sent to Auschwitz on May 18, 1944, where he perished.

Page 26 MAN WITH A LONG BEARD

Pencil drawing on tinted paper (archive number 129774). Signed "MEITNER EVA" in lower left corner.

Eva Meitnerová was born in Prostějov on May 1, 1931, and deported to Terezin on July 4, 1942. Another 22 of her drawings, mainly pencil sketches and pastels, are included in the collection. One of the most interesting is the pastel "Seder," depicting a holiday supper during Passover in which the children had participated in their homes. In Terezin she lived in house number 14 and belonged to Group IV. She died on October 28, 1944, in Auschwitz.

Page 27 TREE

Detail from a watercolor on tinted paper (archive number 129394). It is signed "I. Ruth Čech" in the lower right corner.

For biographical note on Ruth Čechová see catalog entry for p. 76.

Page 29 DWELLINGS IN TEREZIN

A watercolor on tinted paper (archive number 129406). On the upper right corner it is signed "Hana Grünfeld. VI. 1944 4B."

Hana Grünfeldová was born on May 20, 1935, place unknown, and deported to Terezin on December 14, 1941. She has 9 more drawings included in the collection, most of them dating between April and June 1944. She lived in Block IV at Terezin and perished at Auschwitz in 1944.

Page 31 ROOM WITH BUNKBED

Pencil and watercolor drawing (archive number 121976), signed across the top edge of the paper "Erika Taussig IV b 24.V.1944."

Erika Taussigová was born in Prague on October 28, 1934, and was deported to Terezin on December 17, 1941. She is represented in the collection with 15 other drawings, most of them pastels and watercolors, dated between April and June 1944. From the careful inscriptions on her drawings we learn that Erika lived in house number CIII and later in Block IV. One of the most interesting of her drawings is "Heart with a Horseshoe," dedicated to her teacher Friedl Dicker-Brandeis with the inscription "Fir frau Brandajs-Erika" and dated April 8, 1944. She died at Auschwitz on October 16, 1944.

Page 33 **AMBULANCE**

A pencil drawing (archive number 124736), signed on back "Ilona Weissová Pokoj 13.h.18."

Ilona Weissová was born on March 6, 1932, and deported to Terezin from Prague on December 14, 1941. She was sent to Auschwitz on May 15, 1944, where she perished.

Page 35 **FANTASY**

Pasted paper collage on office form (archive number 129466) reproduced vertically. Signed "Lissauová Hana heim 28 5 2. III" on reverse side.

Hana Lissauová was born on February 4, 1930, in Lany and deported to Terezin on February 25, 1942. She has 22 additional drawings in the collection, mostly pencil sketches based on themes suggested by her teacher. Two drawings date from February and May 1944. She lived in house number 28 at Terezin and belonged to Group A. She perished at Auschwitz on October 16, 1944.

Page 36 **FIGURES OF LITTLE GIRLS**

Right half of a drawing. It is a pencil sketch done on writing paper (archive number 129412). On left corner it is signed "JANA HELLEROVÁ 6 Roku, C III i h."

Jana Hellerová was born on February 3, 1938, in Prague and deported to Terezin on July 15, 1943. She was the youngest pupil in the Terezin "school." She has one other pencil drawing in the collection. She died on October 16, 1944, at Auschwitz.

Page 37 **MAN WITH A MUSTACHE**

Paper cutout with brown paint (archive number 133420).

Hanuš Klauber was born on May 12, 1932, and deported to Terezin from Plzeň on January 18, 1942. He was sent to Auschwitz on September 28, 1944, where he perished.

Page 38 **BIRD AND BUTTERFLY**

A paper collage with watercolor and pencil (archive number 129765). The artist is unknown.

Page 40 **Dancing Children**

Watercolor on gray paper (archive number 129963). Signed on right side: "Helena Schanzerová 2 skupina 2 III."

Helena Schanzerová was born in Prague on November 3, 1933, and deported to Terezin on July 30, 1942. She has 6 more drawings in the collection. At Terezin Helena lived in building CIII, house number 13, and belonged to Group I. She died on May 18, 1944, in Auschwitz.

Page 42 **BARRACKS**

A pencil drawing (archive number 133061), signed in upper right corner "IV" and "Wollsteinerová, Eva."

Eva Wollsteinerová was born on January 24, 1931, and deported to Terezin

from Brno on April 8, 1942. She was sent to Auschwitz on October 23, 1944, where she perished.

Page 43 **NIGHT SKY**

Collage of paper cutouts of office forms pasted on shiny background (archive number 121586).

Helena Mändlová was born in Prague on May 21, 1930, and deported to Terezin on December 17, 1941. There are 8 more of her drawings in the collection. One of the most interesting is a pencil sketch labeling the children's homes, shops, and other buildings at Terezin. She lived in building L410, house number 28. She was a student of Friedl Dicker-Brandeis. She died on December 18, 1943, in Auschwitz.

Pages **ABSTRACT**
44–45

Watercolor on the gray cover of a sketchbook (archive number 125420). Signed "SILVÍN VI. 25. VI. 1944" at bottom.

Nely Silvínová was born in Prague on December 21, 1931, and deported to Terezin on August 10, 1942. Sixteen more of her drawings are in the collection, most dating between April and June 1944. At Terezin she lived in house number 14 and belonged to Group V. She was a student of Friedl Dicker-Brandeis. She died on October 4, 1944, in Auschwitz.

Page 46 **MENORAH**

A drawing done in pastels on the reverse side of a piece of semiglossy yellow paper (archive number 129209). On the upper left corner is inscribed "Karpeles Ireni."

Irena Karpelesová was born in Prague on December 30, 1930, and deported to Terezin on December 22, 1942. She has 27 other drawings included in this collection, their themes suggested either by her teacher or chosen by herself and reflecting life in Terezin and its environs. At Terezin, Irena lived in house number 13 and belonged to Group A. She died on October 32, 1944, in Auschwitz.

Page 47 **DWELLINGS IN TEREZIN**

A pencil drawing done on gray cardboard (archive number 129407). Signature on back of drawing: "NOVÁK J. X 1943 13 stunde."

For biographical note on Josef Novák see catalog entry for p. 16.

Pages **PASSOVER SEDER**
48–49

A crayon and pencil drawing (archive number 129947) signed in the lower right corner "Doris Weiser."

Doris Weiserová was born on May 17, 1932, and deported to Terezin from Olomouc on June 30, 1942. She was sent to Auschwitz on October 4, 1944, where she perished.

Pages **GIRL LOOKING OUT OF THE WINDOW**
50–51

Watercolor on tinted paper (archive number 129389). Signature on reverse side: "Nina Ledererová I III."

Nina Ledererová was born September 7, 1931, in Prague and deported to Terezin on September 8, 1942. She has 9 other drawings in the collection of children's art from Terezin, most of which were based on assigned themes. They date from April to May 1944. She was a member of Group II. Her last drawings, "Flower Study" and "Sketch," were done on May 9, 1944. She died in Auschwitz on May 15, 1944.

Page 52 **BUILDING AT NIGHT**

A watercolor (archive number 129214) signed in lower right corner "Polach Dity."

Dita Polachová was born on July 12, 1929. She was deported to Terezin on November 20, 1942, and deported to Auschwitz on December 18, 1943. She was liberated from Bergen-Belsen in May 1945. Dita Kraus now lives in Netanya, Israel.

Page 53 **STARLIGHT IN DARK ROOM**

Crayon and pencil drawing (archive number 129065) signed "S. S. Spitzová" in lower right corner.

Soňa Spitzová was born on February 17, 1931, and deported to Terezin from Prague on December 10, 1941. She was sent to Auschwitz on October 6, 1944, where she perished.

Page 54 **GUARD WITH STICK**

A collage of paper cut from an office ledger (archive number 125499) signed across top with "Soňa Spitzová."

For biographical note on Soňa Spitzová see catalog entry for p. 53.

Pages **SAILBOAT**
56–57 Watercolor (archive number 173143) with no signature.

Page 59 **SUNSET**

Watercolor (archive number 133162) with no signature.

Helga Polláková was born on December 11, 1928, and deported to Terezin on May 15, 1943. She was deported again on December 19, 1944. Her fate is unknown.

Page 60 **MAN ON A BOAT**

Pastels on tinted paper (archive number 129061). Inscription in upper right: "Elly HELLER 28. III 1944."

Elly Hellerová was born in Prague on September 15, 1930, and deported to Terezin on December 22, 1942. Eight more of her drawings from the first half of 1944 appear in the collection. She belonged to Group IV. She perished in Auschwitz on October 6, 1944.

Page 63 **BUSY STREET SCENE**

Watercolor, crayon, and pencil on paper (archive number 129005) signed "Eva Brunner 10 . . . [not readable]" in upper left corner.

Eva Brunnerová was born on August 27, 1933, and deported to Terezin from Brno on March 19, 1942. She was sent to Auschwitz on May 18, 1944, and perished there.

Pages **CHILDREN IN THE PARK**
64–65 A pencil sketch on tinted paper (archive number 129950). The upper left corner is marked "G. Frei (I) XIII III 11 Jahre."

Gabriela Freiová was born on January 1, 1933, in Holice in Bohemia and was deported to Terezin on December 9, 1942.

See catalog entry for p. 1 for biographical note.

Page 66 **LEAVES OF A TREE**
Detail from lower right portion of drawing "Study of Leaves," a black watercolor done on tinted paper (archive number 131120). Signed on upper right corner "Biennenfeld Milan Heim II."

Milan Biennenfeld was born in Prague on March 28, 1930, and deported to Terezin on October 24, 1942. He has one more pencil sketch included in the collection of children's art from Terezin, where he was a member of class 10. He lived in boys' dormitory II at Terezin. He died May 18, 1944, at Auschwitz.

Page 67 **CAMEL**
A pencil drawing (archive number 133456) signed in lower right "Karel Sattler IV b 31 V 1944" upside down.

Karel Sattler was born on November 16, 1932, and arrived in Terezin on September 8, 1942. He was deported from Terezin on October 4, 1944.

Page 68 **MAN STANDING ALONE**
Collage (archive number 129740) with no signature.

Page 71 **HOUSE WITH GARDEN**
A watercolor painted on the reverse side of a piece of shiny red paper (archive number 129499). Signed in lower right corner "IV sku. Langová Marianna."

Marianna Langová was born in Prague on February 27, 1932, and deported to Terezin on July 2, 1942. The collection of children's art from Terezin contains an additional 14 of her drawings dated between April and May 1944. She lived in house number 13 at Terezin and belonged to Group IV. She died on October 6, 1944, in Auschwitz.

Pages **PARADISE—FORBIDDEN FRUIT**
72–73 Pencil drawing (archive number 129889).

Eva Heská was born in Přerov on May 29, 1930, and deported to Terezin on June 26, 1942. Nineteen other drawings of hers are in the Terezin children's collection, dating from February to May 1944. She lived in house number 13 at Terezin and belonged to Group IV. She died on May 18, 1944, in Auschwitz.

Page 75 GIRL WITH RAISED FISTS

A pencil sketch on tinted paper (archive number 125433). On the lower right corner there is a notation in the handwriting of her teacher Friedl Dicker-Brandeis: "Raja 25."

Raja Engländerová was born in Prague on August 25, 1929, and deported to Terezin on January 30, 1942. The collection of children's art from Terezin contains 23 more of her drawings, mostly watercolors and pencil sketches. She was among the talented pupils, drawing mainly from her own chosen themes. Part of the drawings are dated from April to May 1944. In Terezin she lived in house number 25. After the liberation she returned to Prague.

Page 76 GARDEN

Watercolor on tinted paper (archive number 129394). It is signed "I. Ruth Čech" in the lower right corner.

Ruth Čechová was born in Brno on April 19, 1931, and brought to Terezin on March 19, 1943. She has 13 more drawings, pastels, watercolors, and pencil sketches included in this collection, most of which are dated between April and June 1944. At Terezin Ruth lived in house number CIII and was a member of Group I. She died at Auschwitz on October 19, 1944.

Page 79 SCALING THE MOUNTAINS

A crayon and pencil drawing (archive number 131054) signed in lower right corner "Eva Schurová L 4 7 [letter not readable] II."

Eva Schurová was born on June 2, 1935, and deported to Terezin from Pardubice on December 9, 1942. She was sent to Auschwitz on May 15, 1944, where she perished.

Pages LANDSCAPE WITH TREES
80–81

Drawing in pencil and pastels on reverse of semiglossy yellow paper (archive number 129812). Signature in upper left: "Ela Kestler I."

Ela Kestlerová was born in Prague on July 23, 1933, and deported to Terezin on April 28, 1942. She is represented with 4 more drawings in this collection. One of these is dated 25.IV. (1944). In Terezin she lived in house number 13 and belonged to Group I. She died on October 23, 1944, in Auschwitz.

Page 82 SUN

Detail from upper half of drawing "Landscape with Trees" by Ela Kestlerová. See previous entry.

Page 95 TRAINS

Detail from crayon drawing (archive number 129005) by Eva Brunnerová. See catalog entry for p. 63.

Page GHETTO GUARD
100

Detail from "Impressions from Life at Terezin." It is done in pencil on the back of a piece of glossy red paper (archive number 129408). In the upper right corner is written "Weisskopf S VII X."

Alfred Weisskopf was born on January 24, 1932, in Prague and deported to Terezin on December 22, 1942. He has 6 more drawings in this collection of children's art from Terezin, and these are among the most interesting because they take their themes from Terezin itself and its environs. He lived in building L417, house number 10. He perished December 18, 1944, in Auschwitz.

Page
106

FLOWERS WITH BUTTERFLY

Detail from "Butterflies" (archive number 129979) by Marika Friedmanová. For biographical note see catalog entry for p. iii.

Cover

VIEW OF TEREZIN

Paper collage (archive number 131296) by Hanuš Weinberg. For biographical note see catalog entry for p. 15.

CATALOG OF POEMS

The originals of these poems by the children of Terezin are in the archives of the State Jewish Museum in Prague. They were turned over to the museum on November 3, 1952, by Mrs. A. Flachová of Brno, and were part of the property of her husband, who had been a teacher in one of the Terezin children's homes, L417. There are 42 of these manuscripts, and in typed copy, 24. The folio in which the poems were given bears the following inscription: TEREZIN 1941–1945. The folio evidently dates from a later period. It contained those poems listed in the archive under the number 108218. A copy of the poem "Fear," by Eva Picková, was given to the State Jewish Museum in 1955 by Dr. R. Feder. The prose of Petr Fischl, "The Diary of Pavel Bondy," archive number 101517/55, is deposited in the museum archive in typed copy and was donated during the museum's documentation campaign in 1945, when written records and memoirs from the former Terezin ghetto were collected.

Page 1 **THE BUTTERFLY**

Quotation from Pavel Friedmann's poem "The Butterfly." For further facts see catalog entry for p. 39.

Page 3 **AT TEREZIN**

A children's rhyme written in pencil on a piece of drawing paper. The handwriting is simple, childish, and there are no grammatical errors. It is signed "Teddy" in the right corner; "1943" and "L410" have been added in another handwriting. The author's name cannot be determined, but he was probably a member of the same group as Miroslav Košek, with whom he lived in children's home L410.

Pages 4–5 **THE CLOSED TOWN**

The poem is preserved in a typewritten copy. All other facts are unknown.

Page 6 **WE GOT USED TO STANDING . . .**

Excerpt from the prose of Petr Fischl in "Diary of Pavel Bondy." The typed copy is written on a piece of thin copy paper and was donated to the State Jewish Museum during its documentation campaign.

Petr Fischl was born in Prague on September 9, 1929, and deported to Terezin on December 8, 1943. He died at Auschwitz on October 8, 1944. His work is lyrical prose, but his description of Terezin is exceptional for its accuracy and sober tone.

Page 9 **THE OLD HOUSE**

Franta (František) Bass was born in Brno on September 4, 1930. He was deported to Terezin on December 2, 1941, and died in Auschwitz on October 28, 1944. Five of his poems are included in this volume. (See pp. 10–11, 30, 57, and 70.)

Pages　**HOME**
10–11　Franta Bass. For biographical note see previous entry.

Page 13 **IT ALL DEPENDS ON HOW YOU LOOK AT IT**

A children's rhyme in two stanzas, written in pen on a German office form. There is the following signature in the upper left corner: "Mir. Košek." The poem is written in a child's script without grammatical errors.

Miroslav Košek was born on March 30, 1932, at Hořelice in Bohemia and deported to Terezin on February 15, 1942. He died on October 19, 1944 at Auschwitz. At Terezin he lived in children's home L410.

Page 14 **MAN PROPOSES, GOD DISPOSES**

Children's rhyme written in pen on a German office form. It is signed "Koleba: Košek, Löwy, Bachner" in the upper right corner. In the left corner, "26/II" is written in a different script. The rhyme is in a childish handwriting with grammatical errors that have been corrected in pencil by someone else.

For biographical data on Miroslav Košek, see previous entry. No information about Bachner could be found. The third author, Hanuš Löwy, was born in Ostrava on June 29, 1931, and deported to Terezin on September 30, 1942. He died in Auschwitz on October 4, 1944.

Page 17 **TEREZIN**

This poem is preserved in a typewritten copy. The date "1944" is written in pencil in the upper right corner. In the seventh line, the words "two years" have been altered in brown pencil to "four years." In the lower right corner is the pencil signature "Mif."

Pages　**TEREZIN**
20–21　The poem is preserved in a typewritten copy. In the right corner, "IX. 1944" is written in, and on the right side, the following is written in pencil: "Written by children from the ages of 10 to 16, living in homes L318 and L417." The poem is unsigned. The author was identified by O. Klein, former teacher at Terezin, as Hanuš Hachenburg.

Hanuš Hachenburg was born in Prague on July 12, 1929, and deported to Terezin on October 24, 1942. He died on December 18, 1943, in Auschwitz.

Pages　**LIGHTS OUT**
22 and　Excerpts from the Diary of Helga Weissová. Helga Weissová was born in
24　Prague on November 10, 1929. She was deported to Terezin with her parents on December 17, 1941. A gifted artist at the age of 12, she recorded what she saw during her two and a half years at Terezin both in her diary and in her drawings. She was sent to Auschwitz with her mother on October 4, 1944, and, later, to the work camps of Freiberg and Mauthausen. She survived and returned to Prague, where she studied painting with the Czech artist Emil Filla. Helga Weissová-Hošková lives and is an artist in Prague.

Page 27 **YES, THAT'S THE WAY THINGS ARE**
Children's rhyme in two stanzas written in pen on a German office form. The signature at the bottom reads "Koleba: Košek, Löwy, Bachner." It is written in a child's script without grammatical errors. For further data see catalog entry for p. 14.

Page 28 **PAIN STRIKES SPARKS ON ME, THE PAIN OF TEREZIN**
This poem is preserved in manuscript form written in pen on a piece of paper torn out of a notebook. There are 3 other poems on this same sheet of paper, one of which is crossed out. From the letters it seems probable that it is a copy. No biographical data are available.

Page 30 **ILLNESS**
Poem by Franta Bass. See catalog entry for p. 9 for biographical note.

Page 32 **THERESIENSTADT'S HOSPITAL**
Anonymous.

Page 34 **CONCERT IN THE OLD SCHOOL GARRET**
The poem is preserved in typewritten copy; "played by Gideon Klein" is written in pencil in the upper right corner. No other data.

Pages **A LETTER TO DADDY**
36–37 Anonymous.

Page 39 **THE BUTTERFLY**
The poem is preserved in typewritten copy on thin copy paper in the collection of poetry by Pavel Friedmann, which was donated to the State Jewish Museum during its documentation campaign (archive number 101516, 1–8). It is dated June 4, 1942, in the left corner.
Pavel Friedmann was born on January 7, 1921, in Prague and deported to Terezin on April 26, 1942. He died in Auschwitz on September 29, 1944.

Pages **THE LITTLE MOUSE**
40–41 A children's verse written in pen on a German office form and having two stanzas. "Koleba: Košek, Löwy, Bachner" is written in the right corner, and above it in pencil, "26/II." The handwriting is that of a child and there are no grammatical errors. For further facts see catalog entry for p. 14.

Pages **AN EVENING IN TEREZIN**
42–43 Eva Schulzová was born on July 20, 1931. She died in Auschwitz on December 18, 1943.

Pages **HOMESICK**
46–47 The poem is preserved in manuscript and is written in pencil on a sheet of lined paper torn from a notebook. The date "9. III. 1943" is in the upper right corner. All other facts are missing.

Page 50 **I'D LIKE TO GO ALONE**

Preserved in manuscript and written in pencil on a scrap of yellowed paper. On the other side is the inscription "Alena Synková" in ink.

Alena Synková was born in Prague on September 24, 1926, and deported to Terezin on December 22, 1942. She returned home after the liberation. Four of her poems are included in this volume. (See pp. 61, 69, and 74.)

Pages **NIGHT IN THE GHETTO**
52–53
The poem is preserved in manuscript and is written in pen on a sheet of white paper, together with three more poems by the same author. At the bottom underneath the poem in the middle of the page is the date "1943" and on the other side "L410" written by a different hand in pencil. All other information is lacking.

Page 55 **FEAR**

The poem is preserved in a copy turned over to the State Jewish Museum in Prague by Dr. R. Feder in 1955. It is signed at the bottom, "twelve-year-old Eva Picková from Nymburk."

Eva Picková was born in Nymburk on May 15, 1929, and deported to Terezin on April 16, 1942; she perished in Auschwitz on December 18, 1943.

Page 57 **I AM A JEW**

Franta Bass. See catalog entry for p. 9 for biographical note.

Page 58 **DUSK**

Anonymous.

Page 61 **TO OLGA**

The poem is preserved in manuscript and is written in pencil on a scrap of lined paper. It is not signed; at the end of the poem is the number of one of the children's homes, "L410." From the handwriting and style it was probably written by Alena Synková (for biographical data see catalog entry for p. 50).

Page 62 **PREPARING FOR THE COMMISSION'S VISIT**

Excerpt from the diary of Helga Weissová. For biographical note see catalog entry for p. 22.

Page 65 **FORGOTTEN**

The poem is preserved in manuscript and is written in pen on a square piece of paper torn from a notebook. There is a spelling error in the title. All other information is missing.

Pages **CAMPFIRE**
66–67
Anna Lindtová was born on March 19, 1930. She was deported to Terezin from Prague on May 12, 1942. She died in Auschwitz on October 28, 1944.

Page 69 **UNTITLED**

Alena Synková. For biographical data see catalog entry for p. 50.

***Page 70* THE GARDEN**

The poem is preserved in manuscript, probably a copy, together with 7 other poems. There is the signature "Franta Bass" on the right side. For biographical note on Franta Bass see catalog entry for p. 9.

***Page 74* TEARS**

Alena Synková. For biographical data see catalog entry for p. 50.

***Page 77* ON A SUNNY EVENING**

The poem is preserved in a typewritten copy. There is the date "1944" in the upper right corner. No more facts are available.

***Page 78* THE STORM**

Jirka (Jiri) Polak was born on February 20, 1925. He was deported from Prague to Terezin on August 3, 1942, and to Auschwitz on September 29, 1944. He survived the war.

***Pages* BIRDSONG**
80–81 The poem is preserved in manuscript and is written in pen on a sheet of white paper together with the poem "Night in the Ghetto" (see pp. 52–53).

***Page 83* BIRDSONG II**

The poem is preserved in manuscript and is written in pen on a square piece of paper torn from a notebook, together with three other poems. Judging from the handwriting and the paper, it is by the same author as the poem "Forgotten" (see p. 65).

EPILOGUE
by Jiri Weil

In Czechoslovakia there is a strange place called Terezin, some 60 kilometers from Prague. It was founded by order of Emperor Joseph II of Austria 200 years ago and was named after his mother, Maria Theresa. This walled-in fortress was constructed on plans drafted by Italian military engineers and has 12 ramparts that enclose the town in the shape of a star. It was to have been a fortress and it became a sleepy army garrison dominated by the barracks, where the homes of the inhabitants were a necessary nuisance. There were homes, taverns, a post office, a bank, and a brewery. There was a church as well, built in a sober style and belonging to the barracks as part of the army community. The little town seemed to have been forced onto the countryside, a lovely countryside without either high mountains or dizzy cliffs, without deep ravines or swift rivers . . . only blue hills, green meadows, fruit trees, and tall poplars.

Today a shadow still lingers above this little town, as though funeral wagons still drive along its streets, as though the dust stirred by a thousand footsteps still eddies in the town square. Today it seems sometimes as though from every corner, from every stairway and from every corridor, peer human faces, gaunt, exhausted, with eyes full of fear.

During the war years, Terezin was a place of famine and of fear. Somewhere far away, in Berlin, men in uniforms had held meetings. These men decided to exterminate all the Jews in Europe, and because they were used to doing things thoroughly, with the calculated, cool passion of a murderer, they worked out plans in which they fixed the country, the place, and the timetable as well as the stopping places on that road to death. One of those stopping places was Terezin.

It was meant to be a model camp that foreigners could be shown, and it was termed a ghetto. At first, Jews from Bohemia and Moravia were brought to Terezin, but finally they came from all over Europe and from there were shipped farther east to the gas chambers and ovens. Everything in this small town was false, invented; every one of its inhabitants was condemned in advance to die. It was only a funnel without an outlet. Those who contrived this trap and put it on their map, with its fixed timetable of life and death, knew all about it. They knew its future as well. Those who were brought there in crowded railroad coaches and cattle cars after days and days of cruelty, of humiliation, of offense, of beatings, and of theft knew very little about it. Some of them believed the murderers' falsehoods, that they could sit out the war here in quiet safety. Others came to Terezin already crushed, yet with a spark of hope that, even so, perhaps they might escape their destiny. There were also those who knew that Terezin was only one station on a short

timetable and that is why they tried so hard to keep at least themselves alive and perhaps their family. And those who were good and honorable endeavored to keep the children alive, the aged and the ailing. All were finally deceived, and the same fate awaited all of them.

But the children who were brought there knew nothing. They came from places where they had already known humiliation. They had been expelled from the schools. They had sewn stars on their hearts, on their jackets and blouses, and were allowed to play only in the cemeteries. That wasn't so bad, if you look at it with the eyes of a child, even when they heard their parents' lamentations, even when they heard strange words charged with horror such as mapping, registration, and transport. When they were herded with their parents into the ghetto, when they had to sleep on the concrete floors in crowded garrets or clamber up three-tiered bunks, they began to look around and quickly understood the strange world in which they had to live. They saw reality, but they still maintained a child's outlook, an outlook of truth that distinguishes between night and day and cannot be confused with false hopes and the shadow play of an imaginary life.

And so they lived, locked within walls and courtyards. This was their world, a world of color and shadow, of hunger and of hope.

The children played in the barracks yard and the courtyards of the onetime homes. Sometimes they were permitted to breathe a little fresh air upon the ramparts. From the age of 14, they had to work, to live the life of an adult. Sometimes they went beyond the walls to work in the gardens, and they were no more considered to be children. The smaller ones acted out their fairy tales and even children's operas. But they did not know that they, too, as well as the grownups, had been used deceitfully, in an effort to convince a commission of foreigners from the Red Cross that Terezin was a place where adults and children alike could live. Secretly, they studied and they drew pictures. Three months, half a year, one or two years, depending on one's luck, because transports came and went continually, headed east into nothingness.

From these 15,000 children, who for a time played and drew pictures and studied, only 100 came back. They saw everything that grownups saw. They saw the endless lines in front of the canteens, they saw the funeral carts used to carry bread and the human beings harnessed to pull them. They saw the infirmaries that seemed like a paradise to them and funerals that were only a gathering up of coffins. They saw executions, too, and were perhaps the only children in the world who captured them with pencil and paper. They heard the shouts of the SS men at roll call and the meek mumblings of prayer in the barracks where the grownups lived.

But the children saw, too, what the grownups didn't want to see—the beauties beyond the village gates, the green meadows and the bluish hills, the ribbon of highway reaching off into the distance and the imagined road marker pointing toward Prague, the animals, the birds, the butterflies—all this was beyond the village walls and they could look at it only from afar, from the

barracks windows, and from the ramparts of the fort. They saw things, too, that grownups cannot see—princesses with coronets, evil wizards and witches, jesters and bugs with human faces, a land of happiness where for an admission of one crown, there was everything to be had—cookies, candy, a roast stuck with a fork from which soda pop trickled. They saw, too, the rooms they'd lived in at home, with curtains at the window and a kitten and a saucer of milk. But they transported it to Terezin. There had to be a fence and a lot of pots and pans, because pots and pans were supposed to be filled with food.

All this they drew and painted and many other things besides; they loved to paint and draw, from morning till evening.

But when they wrote poems, it was something else again. Here one finds words about "painful Terezin," about "the little girl who got lost." These told of longings to go away somewhere where there are kinder people; there are old grandfathers gnawing stale bread and rotten potatoes for lunch, there was a "longing for home" and fear. Yes, fear came to them and they could tell of it in their poems, knowing that they were condemned. Perhaps they knew it better than the adults.

There were 15,000 of them, and 100 came back. You are looking at their drawings now after many years, when that world of hunger, fear, and horror seems to us almost like a cruel fairy tale about evil wizards, witches, and cannibals. The drawings and poems—that is all that is left of these children, for their ashes have long since sifted across the fields around Auschwitz. Their signatures are here and some of the drawings are inscribed with the year, and the number of their group. Of those who signed their names, it has been possible to find out a few facts: the year and place of their birth, the number of their transport to Terezin and to Auschwitz, and then the year of their death. For most of them, it was 1944, the next-to-last year of World War II.

But their drawings and their poems speak to us; these are their voices that have been preserved, voices of reminder, of truth, and of hope.

We are publishing them not as dry documents out of thousands of such witnesses in a sea of suffering, but to honor the memory of those who created these colors and these words. That's the way these children probably would have wanted it when death overtook them.

AFTERWORD
by Vaclav Havel

The suffering of an innocent and vulnerable child always evokes sorrow in an adult. But if such pain is caused intentionally, then it represents a breakdown of reason and conscience, loss of integrity, and the total absence of feeling. How else to explain the acts of Nazi torturers who abducted Jewish children—with their parents or by themselves—and sent them to the Terezin concentration camp? Statistics and various documents tell us about their misery, killing, and death. As Jiri Weil writes in his Epilogue, of these 15,000 children, only 100 came back.

With a heavy heart I have more than once encountered the delicate testimony of the longings, dreams, and experiences of the Terezin children. They take me back to a time when our country was occupied by the Nazis, when the world was at war, and I as a young boy was learning about fear, humiliation, and defiance. These drawings also aroused in me something akin to shame for something I could do nothing about: for the fact that my Jewish classmates were not allowed to go to school, that they were coerced into wearing a Star of David on their clothes so to distinguish them from the others, that they were deported, and finally because I survived but my peers did not.

I still read the poems of children from Terezin. They are full of longing for a world different from the miserable life they led, a longing for games and freedom, for gentleness and beauty. Death, which was so close, appears only between the lines. I also look at their drawings. There is only a shadow of grief and anxiety in them, there is much more about dreams of spring, of flowers, butterflies, birds, and also a great longing to be happy and carefree. The souls of these children used poems and drawings as a defense, sometimes by giving vent to anxiety and at other times by depicting a dream.

The gentle traces of the children in the Terezin concentration camp continue to be, by their scope and impact, an expressive testimony in our day.

CHRONOLOGY

1939 March 15	German Wehrmacht enters Prague. Establishment of Protectorate of Bohemia and Moravia. Up to this time, Jewish children attended the state elementary schools.
July 26	"Central Office for Jewish Resettlement" set up. A census of Jewish inhabitants was immediately begun according to racial law.
December 1	Jewish children excluded from state elementary schools.
1940 June 14	Auschwitz concentration camp set up.
1941 September 27	Reinhard Heydrich named acting Reichsprotector. One of his first acts was to order the mass deportation of Jews and the establishment of Terezin as a Jewish ghetto.
October 16	First transport leaves Prague for Lodz ghetto. Among them were children.
October 19	Terezin turned into a Jewish ghetto. In 1930 it had 7,181 inhabitants, half of whom were military personnel living in 11 barracks.
1942 January 9– October 26	Transports begin to leave for eastern destinations, averging 1,000 people, among them children. Of these, 1 in 100 returned.
August 31	Terezin had a population of 41,552 prisoners. There was 1.6 square meters of space for each person. The average workweek was from 80 to 100 hours. Children from the age of 14 were subject to compulsory labor the same as adults. From 106 to 156 persons died every day.
December 6	There were 3,541 children living in Terezin, 2,000 of whom lived in children's "homes."
1943 December 31	There were 3,367 children in Terezin, 1,969 living in children's "homes."
1944 December 31	At Terezin 819 children were counted under the age of 15 years.
1945 May 7	Terezin liberated by Soviet Army.

*A total of around 15,000 children
under the age of 15 passed through Terezin.
Of these, around 100 came back.*